Saul Vaigers by
William Hershaw and Les McConnell
Published by Grace Note Publications 2021

ISBN 978-1-913162-13-9

SAUL VAIGERS

Thocht up, screivit and pentit by twaa halie brithers
William Hershaw & Les McConnell

2021

January	February	March
Kentigern	Margaret Sinclair	St. Cuthbert

April	May	June
Martyrs	St Joseph	Colmcille

July	August	September
Drostan	Fiacre	Ninian

October	November	December
Regulus	Margaret	Barbara

A Calendar of Saints, each related to Scotland, its medieval shrines and pilgrims' routes

Solvitur Ambulando I

Found in a medieval midden:
a fallen pilgrim's badge,
broken, time-bent, the half missing
but knowable after centuries,
after the wearer's setting out,
after the wearer's wearing away.

A life token that may be redeemed.

Kentigern

Kentigern aka Mungo lived in the late sixth century in the Kingdom of Strathclyde. He is the patron saint of Glasgow but he is associated also with Culross in Fife where a medieval Cistercian Abbey was founded many years after his death by Malcolm the First in 1217. Culross is one of the two starting points of The Pilgrim's Way which follows a medieval pilgrims' route through Fife and ends at St Andrews. Kentigern is associated with a number of miracles including the one referred to below when he brought a robin back to life that had been decapitated by school boys.

13th January

cannily you amend
the torn head
to bloodied breast

with gentle hand making
a miraculous rejoinder
to man's cruelty

through the silenced
throat pipe flows
the first voice of the day

Margaret Sinclair

Margaret Anne Sinclair, also known as Sister Mary Francis of the Five Wounds, was born in Edinburgh in 1900 in Middle Arthur Place, in a basement flat of a tenement. She was one of six children of Andrew and Elizabeth Sinclair. Her father was a dustman for Edinburgh City Corporation and her upbringing was typical of many impoverished working class people of the time. She became a Roman Catholic nun, and was noted for her life of prayer and hard work on behalf of her order as well as the poor and vulnerable. She died of tuberuculosis of the throat in London, England, 1925. She was declared "Venerable" by Pope Paul VI on 6th February 1978.

6th February

factory girl
trade unionist
saturday dancer
allotmenteer

cheerful giver
sister of the poor
dinnae-gie-inner

Cuthbert and the Otters

When Saint Cuthbert tired of the company of the monks at Lindisfarne Priory he took to meditating on a small island cut off from the shore. Legend tells that he would pray during the night hours, immersed up to his neck in the freezing waters of the North Sea. As the sun rose, sensing his holiness, otters would appear and rub themselves against his feet.

20th March

a writhing, a twisting
in a white glinting of sun something
flops over beaded stone knots

pulled from the sea of time
a wide-eyed soul agape
with bloodied flank ripped

a small grey brother prays
before the altar of cold feet
God's breakfast brought

Martyrs

Dietrich Bonhoeffer was a German Lutheran pastor, theologian and anti-Nazi dissident. He was accused of being part of the July bomb plot to kill Hitler and hanged on 9th April 1945 at Flossenburg Concentration Camp.

Saint Donnán, Abbot of Eigg, was beheaded on the 17th April in 617 by Vikings after saying Mass.

Saint Magnus of Orkney was killed at Easter on Egilsay on 16th April by his cousin and political rival Hakon, 1117.

Canon Albert Ernest Laurie was a Scottish Episcopalian priest. He won his first Military Cross in 1916 and a second in 1917, both for tending the wounded in the middle of battle, risking his own life. He died in Edinburgh on 25th April, 1937.

St Giles shielded a deer with his body from hunters and was struck by an arrow.

9th April

A month for martyrs:
Donnán at Eigg
Magnus at Egilsay
Bonhoeffer at Flossenburg

A month to mind
the carers and douce axe-tholers
who accept the thorns
in the vicious wood

Cannon Laurie at the Somme
or gentle Saint Giles
who could not bear

a fellow soul to suffer

The chosen selfless ones
who dance in the flame
that draws an inevitable
whirring of wings:

implacable spite

St Joseph the Worker

In 1955 Pope Pius XII ordained the Feast of Saint Joseph the Worker, to be celebrated on the 1st May. This date coincides with the secular International Workers' Day promoted by the Labour Movement since the 1890's, and reflects Joseph's status as patron saint of workers. Catholic and other Christian teachings and stories about Joseph and the Holy Family frequently stress his patience, persistence, courage, and hard work.

1st May

ceaseless shift worker
        carrier of caterpillers
                feeder of mouths
                        saved in the tree:

Joe the Bluetit

Colmcille

"O Columba spes Scotorum...": "O Columba, hope of the Scots..."

14th-century prayer from The Antiphoner of Inchcolm Abbey.

June 9th

bleeding,
the day warrior sinks
into the grave of the West

but tomorrow in the greying East
the turnstone shore
will sing out his resurrection

      tuck, tuck, tuck!

Drostan of Deer

Colmcille, his disciple Drostan, and others, went from Iona into Buchan and established an important missionary centre at Deer on the banks of the Ugie on lands given him by the Mormaer or Pictish ruler of that country. On the death of the Abbot of Dalquhongale (Holywood) some years later, St. Drostan was chosen to succeed him. Later, feeling called to a life of greater seclusion, he resigned his abbacy, went farther north, and became a hermit at Glenesk. The suffering of the poor and needy reduced him to tears, and many miracles are ascribed to him, including the restoration of sight to a priest named Symon.

11th July

tear shedder
sight restorer

sair greeter
een sainer

dropper tear
ath-nuadhachadh sealladh

Fiacre

Saint Fiacre of Breuil (c.600 – August 670), was a Catholic priest, abbot, hermit, and gardener of the seventh century who was famous for his sanctity and skill in curing infirmities. He emigrated from his native Ireland to France, where he made a hermitage together with a vegetable and herb garden, oratory, and hospice for travellers. He is the patron saint of flowers, herbs and gardeners.

11th August

bluebell and blawort
grannie mutch and gowan
sourocks and thistle
heatherbell and harestail

the saul-vaiger's neebors

saul vaiger: soul journeyer, pilgrim; **neebors**: neighbours, companions

Ninian

Ninian (died 432?) is a Christian saint first mentioned in the 8th century as being an early missionary among the Pictish people of what is now Scotland. For this reason he is known as the Apostle to the Southern Picts, and there are numerous dedications to him in those parts of Scotland with a Pictish heritage, throughout the Scottish Lowlands, and in parts of Northern England with a Northumbrian heritage. In Scotland, Ninian is also known as Ringan, and as Trynnian in Northern England. Ninian's major shrine is at Whithorn in Galloway, where he is associated with the Candida Casa (Latin for White House). This marks the end of the 149 mile Whithorn Way which begins in Glasgow.

16th September

grey sky
        cold sea

green hill
        brown path

black shore
        white kirk

cold sky
        grey sea

Regulus

"Quiquidam regulus in sancto andrea et per diocesium eiusdem honoratur."

Regulus or Rule was commanded in a dream by angels to bring Andrew's bones from the Greek city of Patras and sail with them to the far West. Eventually his boat came to shore at Kinrymont in the Pictish Kingdom of Fiobh. The church he founded there became St Andrews Cathedral.

17th October

the dream driven
bone bringer
kirk builder
beyond the West

hoisted
his handsome blue sail
his saltire of hope

Margaret

Margaret came to Scotland in 1068 when the boat she sailed from Northumbria that was bound for the continent was diverted in a storm into the Forth. She landed at what is now St. Margaret's Hope. She married Malcom III. Margaret was known for her piety and charity. She looked after the sick and the poor until her death in 1093. She rose at midnight to pray in her hermitage where the Tower burn runs through Dunfermline Glen. Pope Innocent IV canonized Margaret in 1250 in recognition of her personal holiness, work for ecclesiastical reform, and charity. On 19th June 1250, after her canonisation, her remains were transferred to a chapel in the eastern apse of Dunfermline Abbey. It became a destination for pilgrims.

16th November

Attour the world
saut tears faa dreepan,
bide sauf the nicht,
for God's no sleepin.

An airtless ark
o tint sauls greetin,
bide lown, be sained,
for God's no sleepin.

The daurk maun pass,
the daw comes creepin,
courie doun, courie in,
for God's no sleepin.

attour: across; **saut**: salt; **faa**: fall; **bide**: stay; **sauf**: safe; **tint**: lost; **sauls**: souls; **lown**: peaceful; **sained**: blessed; **maun**: may; **daw**: dawn; **courie**: cuddle.

Barbara

St Barbara the Martyr is the patron saint of miners but also all those who work in dangerous places and conditions. She was an early Christian Greek saint and martyr in the third century. She is associated with lightning (her father was struck by it as a punishment for her murder) and by association with explosions. In some European countries, as a long-standing tradition, one of the first tasks for each new tunnelling project is to establish a small shrine to Santa Barbara at the tunnel entrance. This is often followed with a dedication and an invocation to her asking for protection of the workers.

December 4th

howkers and biggers
saufers thirlt tae mishanter's darg
ask your blessing and beild

beg your shield fae blind blaffs
lichtnen scauds and scarts
and ilka wanchancy dounfaa

in the wards o the airth we pray
here kistit ablaw

howkers: diggers; **saufers**: savers; **thirlt**: chained; **darg**: task; **mishanter**: misfortune; **beild**: protection; **blaff**: blow; **scaud**: burn; **ilka**: each; **wanchancy**: unluckly; **dounfaa**: collapse; **kistit**: boxed, coffined; **ablaw**: below; **airth**: earth.

Solvitur Ambulando II

Ilk vaigin is aye steekit till
the last lanesome path's uncleekit
fae the fankle o gates:

we follae our faithers
ower the hill.

Each journey is always unfinished until
the last lonely path untangles
from the confusion of roads:

we follow our fathers
over the hill.

General Notes

These poems are inspired by three publications:

The Aberdeen Breviary (Latin: Breviarium Aberdonense) is a 16th-century Scottish Catholic breviary. It was the first book to be printed in Edinburgh and in Scotland.

The creation of **The Aberdeen Breviary** is an example of a growing Scottish national identity and cultural confidence at the start of sixteenth century. In 1507, King James IV, commissioned a Scottish version of the **Sarum Breviary**, or Rite, which was English in origin, and had been in use since the twelfth century. As Scotland had no printing press, the booksellers Walter Chepman and Androw Mylar of Edinburgh were given the remit to go abroad and bring one back.

The content of **The Breviary** was devised by William Elphinstone, Bishop of Aberdeen, who had received the King's permission to establish the University of Aberdeen twelve years before, and the Scottish philosopher and historian Hector Boece. They began their work in 1509, and the first copy, produced as a small octavo, came off the press in 1510. Only four copies are extant.

In writing these poems I am indebted to **Saints, Dedications and Cults in Mediaeval Fife** by Giles W. Dove, a thesis submitted for the Degree of MPhil at the University of St Andrews in 1988 and now online. It provides an illuminating account of how popular the cult of sainthood was and describes in some detail the many shrines and sites of veneration that existed at this period.

Finally, **The Fife Pilgrim Way - In the Footsteps of Monks, Miners and Martyrs** by Ian Bradley, published by Birlinn, 2019. I quote: "Saints' shrines drew those seeking healing and relief from pain and suffering, whether physical, mental or spiritual, both for themselves and others." The author explains how the various pre-

Reformation saints' cults enjoyed a popularity and fame akin to modern day celebrities. As well, the book is an invaluable guide through the landscape of Fife and the Pilgrim's Way itself, including accounts of more recent and contemporary lives.

With thanks to Ann McCluskey, Brendan McCluskey, Margaret Bennett for help and encouragement. Special thanks to Gonzalo Mazzei for his editing and book designing skills.

Willie Hershaw & Les McConnell, 2020

A Prayer

Saint Isidore O Seville,
screiver and minder o aa kent things,
tak tent tae intercede on our behauf:
maun ilka howpfou glede,
smaa mickle-byte o our sauls' data
be saufed.

William Hershaw

Poet, playwright, singer and musician. He is a member of the editorial board of **Lallans**. He is the founder of the folk group **The Bowhill Players** who perform music celebrating Fife's Coal Mining culture. In 2018 Grace Note Publications published **The Sair Road**, his Scots language version of the **Stations of the Cross** set during the 1984 Miners' Strike. His poems and songs have been widely published and recorded both in Scotland and abroad.

Resources

<http://www.scottishpoetrylibrary.org.uk/poetry/poets/william-hershaw>

<https://en.wikipedia.org/wiki/William_Hershaw>

<http://www.culturematters.org.uk/index.php/arts/poetry/item/3069-christ-is-a-communist-and-god-is-a-miner-the-sair-road-by-william-hershaw>

<https://en-gb.facebook.com/bowhillplayers/>

Les McConnell

Born in Ayrshire in 1947. He received his art education at Edinburgh College of Art in the 1960's. In 1970 he was awarded a post graduate scholarship spending part of the time in Holland. He has participated in numerous exhibitions including the Royal Scottish Academy, the Society of Scottish Artists and a one man show in Fife. The collaboration with William Hershaw started in 2017 and has proved to be a very successful partnership resulting in a number of publications and exhibitions. Working with William opened a rich seam of visual possibilities, the depth and descriptive quality of his writing make the images leap from the page. This latest work has been an exciting journey into Scotland's past.

Solvitur Ambulando I, 2019
Pen and watercolour
30 x 24 cms

Kentigern, 2019
Pen and watercolour
30 x 24 cms

Margaret Sinclair, 2019
Pen and watercolour
30 x 24 cms

Cuthbert and the Otters, 2019
Pen and watercolour
30 x 24 cms

Martyrs, 2019
Pen and watercolour
30 x 24 cms

St Joseph the Worker, 2019
Pen and watercolour
30 x 24 cms

Colmcille, 2019
Pen and watercolour
30 x 24 cms

Drostan of Deer, 2019
Pen and watercolour
30 x 24 cms

Fiacre, 2019
Pen and watercolour
30 x 24 cms

Ninian, 2019
Pen and watercolour
30 x 24 cms

Regulus, 2019
Pen and watercolour
30 x 24 cms

Margaret, 2019
Pen and watercolour
30 x 24 cms

Barbara, 2019
Pen and watercolour
30 x 24 cms

Solvitur Ambulando II, 2019
Pen and watercolour
30 x 24 cms